Praise for
The Bookshop on
Lafayette Street

"Getting lost in Classics has been a hobby of mine for nearly two decades. Reading this collection is like entering a small, hidden door in the corner of Eric's store and finding a literary fantasyland. This stuff is cool."
—*Jeff Edelstein,* Trentonian

"Just like a Cajun chef making up a good pot of gumbo, *The Bookshop on Lafayette Street* has put together some tasty literary ingredients in this hodge pot. Taste and see!"
—*Todd C.C. Evans, Don Evans Players*

"A joy to read."
—*Lori Johansson, Molly Rhythm*

"I strongly recommend it."
—*Josue Lora, Agudos Clef*

"I can legitimately say after every poem, short story, play 'that was my favorite.' *The Bookshop on Lafayette Street* left me wanting more."
—*Christina Sasso, Trenton Waves Podcast*

"On my second read through, I told myself, 'I'll stop when I hit that inevitable story or poem that isn't exciting.' I sat there for hours and didn't stop until the end."
—*c. a. Shofed, Amphora Studio*

The BOOKSHOP on LAFAYETTE STREET

A Collection of Stories and Poems

Ragged Sky Press
Princeton, New Jersey

Published by Ragged Sky Press
270 Griggs Drive
Princeton, NJ 08540

www.raggedsky.com/

Ragged Sky Press is a 501(c)(3) non-profit organization
under the umbrella of Co-Works, which supports
literary and visual arts in New Jersey.

Book design, front cover art, and interior illustrations
by John Gummere
Back cover art by Leon Rainbow
Edited by Eric Maywar

ISBN 978-1-933974-32-3

Library of Congress Control Number: 2019938769

Text typeset in Adobe Garamond Pro,
with subheads in Helvetica Neue.

Printed on acid-free paper. ∞

Printed in the United States of America

10 9 8 7 6 5 4 3 2 1

Introduction

We never planned to open a bookshop. After buying one man's library to sell at a church sale (and only selling three books), we found ourselves with a living room full of wonderful books. We began selling at Columbus Flea Market early on Sunday mornings—but also found ourselves gathering more books than we sold and still turning a modest profit. Next we hosted house parties to which we invited used bookstore owners, plied them with liquor and sold them boxes of books wholesale for their shops. Eventually we opened a bookshop in New Hope, Pennsylvania, in 2000, and another in Trenton, New Jersey, in 2005—Classics Books.

We never planned to write this book. In 2017, Pulitzer Prize–winning poet Yusef Komunyakaa was working on an epic poem and part of it took place at Classics Books. Independently, I was working on some flash fiction that also took place at Classics Books. We bumped into each other (at Classics Books) and decided that we should collaborate on a collection of poems and stories that all take place at our favorite bookstore. We thought a collection of excellent work with a shared setting—and a shared love of bookstores and the people in them—might be an exciting project. We reached out to some of our favorite writers and artists to make it happen.

If you ever wanted to pull a book from the bookshelf and open a hidden passageway or if you ever wanted the bookseller to lock you in the bookstore overnight, this collection is for you.

There is a story about the five greatest bookstores of all time, another about a woman who brings her date to a bookshop to see how he handles himself around books, and another about the ghosts of books burnt in book burnings. There is a play about the most annoying customer in the world, a story about the bookseller and the troll, and a story about a boy who rode on the tops of trains and what that meant.

First and foremost this collection is a love letter to used bookstores; everything that you love about them is here: books, the sense of wonder and discovery, the cozy clutter, idiosyncratic book lovers, and the feeling that you are in a magic haven buttressed against the cruelties of the world.

Enjoy!

—*Eric Maywar*

Extracts

(supplied by Melville's sub-sub-librarian)

One of the great lies in literature is telling people that the first line of *Moby Dick* is "Call me Ishmael." It isn't. The first lines of *Moby Dick* are the etymology of the word "whale" followed by lots of quotes about the same. This was no accident—it is integral to Melville's scheme—whales and doubloons and quotations. One might as well say, bookstores and books and surfistas.

* * *

"Shoppers in used bookstores get the feeling of magic and wonder, and the anticipation that somewhere in the stacks of their favorite bookshop there is something waiting for them, an echo of the back room of the Bookstore Al-jinn, the sense of hope and possibility, and the wish for the betterment of an imperfect world."
—*Abd Allah ibn Baḥr al-Kinānī al-Baṣrī*

"To my mind there is nothing so beautiful or so provocative as a secondhand bookstore.... To me it is astonishing and miraculous to think that any one of us can poke among the stalls for something to read overnight—and that this something may be the sum of a lifetime of sweat, tears, and genius that some poor, struggling, blessed fellow expended trying to teach us the truth."
—*Lionel Barrymore*

"Bookstores are sensual. Book people are great lovers. These are people happy to take their time with something they love; they feel no need to rush. They will spend hours in bed with no regret. They are sensualists. They enjoy the weight of a book in their hands, the texture of the spine, the smell of its pages."
—*the bookseller*

"In the shop window you have promptly identified the cover with the title you were looking for. Following this visual trail, you have forced your way through the shop past the thick barricade of Books You Haven't Read, which are frowning at you from the tables and shelves, trying to cow you...And thus you pass the outer girdle of ramparts, but then you are attacked by the infantry of Books That If You Had More Than One Life You Would Certainly Also Read But Unfortunately Your Days Are Numbered. With a rapid maneuver you bypass them and move into the phalanxes of the Books You Mean To Read But There Are Others You Must Read First, the Books Too Expensive Now And You'll Wait Till They're Remaindered, the Books Ditto When They Come Out in Paperback, Books You Can Borrow From Somebody, Books That Everybody's Read So It's As If You Had Read Them, Too."
—*Italo Calvino,* If on a winter's night a traveler

"Perhaps that is the best way to say it: printed books are magical, and real bookshops keep that magic alive."
—*Jen Campbell,* The Bookshop Book

"I went to a bookstore and asked the saleswoman, 'Where's the self-help section?' She said if she told me, it would defeat the purpose."
—*George Carlin*

"It is clear that the books owned the shop rather than the other way about. Everywhere they had run wild and taken possession of their habitat, breeding and multiplying, and clearly lacking any strong hand to keep them down."
—*Agatha Christie,* The Clocks

"We all just took the bookstore at its word, because if you couldn't trust a bookstore, what could you trust?"
—*Rachel Cohn,* Dash & Lily's Book of Dares

"What I say is, a town isn't a town without a bookstore. It may call itself a town, but unless it's got a bookstore it knows it's not fooling a soul."
—*Neil Gaiman,* American Gods

"His hands were weak and shaking from carrying far too many books from the bookshop. It was the best feeling."
—*Joseph Gordon-Levitt,* The Tiny Book of Tiny Stories, Vol. 1

"Used bookstores are powder kegs, ready to amplify whatever emotion you have when you enter one. If you are happy, you feel happier. If you feel melancholy, you feel sadder."
—*Andrew Hanton*

"I love / to finger pages, reading marginalia / & weighing the heft in my hands."
—*Yusef Komunyakaa, "The Last Bohemian of Avenue A"*

"The truly wide taste in reading is that which enables a man to find something for his needs on the sixpenny tray outside any secondhand bookshop."
—*C. S. Lewis,* The Four Loves

"Classics Books is part chapel, part candy store and I am seven and my mom has just given me a quarter for penny candy."
—*Sid Manikos*

"Everybody wants to pull a book in a bookstore and discover a secret passageway."
—*Eric Maywar*

"The buying of more books than one can read is nothing less than the soul reaching toward infinity."
—*Edward Newton*

"Used bookstores let you be. It is a better place than a bar or a restaurant. There is no minimum number of drinks to purchase and no hurry to leave a table so more customers could sit. You can exist at your own pace in a bookstore."
—*the old man*

"The cycle has come all the way back around: the little bookstore grew into a big bookstore, which was squashed by the superstore, which folded beneath the Internet store, which made people long for a little bookstore. The whole process took about 13 years."
—*Ann Patchett, "Of Bugs and Books,"* New York Times

"A good bookshop is just a genteel Black Hole that knows how to read."
—*Terry Pratchett,* Guards! Guards!

"Those of us who read because we love it more than anything, who feel about bookstores the way some people feel about jewelers...."
—*Anna Quindlen,* How Reading Changed My Life

"I have a theory that if I took a first date to a bookstore, I would know if he was worth a second date."
—*Samantha Townes*

"Bookstores always remind me that there are good things in this world."
—*Vincent van Gogh*

"I think that I still have it in my heart someday to paint a book-shop with the front yellow and pink in the evening…like a light in the midst of the darkness."
—*Vincent van Gogh*

The Infinite Collection of Unfinished Stories

Eric Maywar

Everybody wants to pull a book in a bookstore and discover a secret passageway.

At one bookstore, it can happen.

For the change in your pocket, the bookstore owner will tell you which book to pull. When you do, the passageway (which is hidden behind the section that features dream interpretations and recipes for chocolate) swings open to reveal the hidden collection of unfinished stories.

The collection is chaos. Hundreds of thousands of books have a title but only blank pages inside, from every time a writer said, "I should write something," and no ideas came. The other books have fragments of ideas—opening lines, stray characters, settings with no plot, random pearls looking for a string. Most books have pages that were made from napkins and the backs of envelopes and scraps of paper carrying every idea that came to somebody on a train, or in a dream, or sitting at a diner.

Some books are filled with just titles of books.
- *Bottleneck Blues*
- *John Henry's Dead*
- *True Love and Other Short Stories*

Other books are filled with opening lines.
- He never stopped questioning the darkness with his hands.
- I live in a world of other people's decisions.
- I took a long look at my life and realized this is how suicides get started.

There are books of settings.
- Winter was slow in releasing its season.
- It was one of those foggy days by the lake where the water forgets what it is and becomes the sky.
- It was night. White clouds blew fast and low along the skyline, as if something was burning on the other side of the world.

Books of characters.
- William used to think that rain was romantic, but during that summer it only kept his window shut.
- She dressed like an optical illusion.
- You know somebody is desperate when they are drinking from the tip jar.
- He wasn't a superstitious man, but he wasn't a fool either.

There are books of dialogue.
- "Don't get excited. I'm not a house of worship."
- "At this point you have smoked me down to my filter."
- "If I could have super powers, I would want to always have exact change. I certainly wouldn't want to read minds; who wants to go in there?"

There are books of ideas.
- The world turns too fast to get everything done, but too slow to notice.
- Infinity makes people giggle.
- Memories are uncertain friends.
- Audiences know what to expect and that's all they are prepared to believe.
- Books full of all the wishes in the world.

There are books of facts that writers hoped they could make a story out of.
- In the 60s, the Russians used to run their lighthouses with nuclear power.
- Every year, as Scotch ages, about 2% evaporates. The brewers call this the angel's dram, or angel's portion.

There are books of new words not yet in any dictionary like mathemagician and earsight.

There are books of words that sounded nice together that the author wasn't sure yet what they meant.
- A potbellied, burnt-iron banshee with a belly full of Scotland.
- The indecipherable language of crowds.
- The church fired the god who lived there.

There are books of metaphors.
- Playing Russian roulette with a 9mm.
- An eighteen-wheeler on a one-way street.
- The emptiness of coffee.

And there are books full of outlines of story ideas.

- The ghost of a theatre that had burnt down in the middle of a movie. Afterwards, the theatre haunts the neighborhood, flickering movies ghostily on nearby walls, trying desperately to finish showing the movie it started.
- A woman time travels into the past to stop a terrible second date.
- The cat cursed my feet and from then on they took me to all the wrong places.
- A man finds a secret back room full of half-finished ideas. But, how do you finish a story about unfinished stories?

Contents

The Five Greatest Bookstores of All Time

Eric Maywar

It is generally acknowledged that five used bookstores were the greatest used bookstores of all time.

The fifth greatest bookstore of all time was the Borges Book Store in Argentina in 1961. Because of quantum refracturing and heteroglossiac magic, the Borges was impossibly filled with an infinite number of books with every possible combination of letters. Because every possible combination of letters was there, this meant that the most beautiful books ever written were in this collection somewhere. However, they were never located because the vast majority of these infinite books were illegible nonsense, random letters thrown in a random order. The bookstore made a grand total of three novelty sales before it went out of business.

The Celestial Temple Bookshop in China during the Tang dynasty was the fourth greatest bookstore of all time. The Celestial Temple Bookshop carried books made of bamboo and printed by woodblock, scrolls bound at one edge. It was wildly successful for many years, until one day the Monkey King grew concerned that this perfect bookstore would one day disappear. More an entity of action than of thoughtful deliberation, the Monkey King, who knew 72 different transformations, turned the entire collection of books and the bookseller into butterflies, which then flew erratically eastward and towards the Heavenly Kingdom.

The third greatest bookstore of all time was, and is, the Book Store of Ashurbanipal, which is rarely seen and even more rarely visited. This store is a ghost, filled with the haints of books that had been burned out of fear and prejudice as far back as the destruction of the booksellers of Elba in 2240 BC. It has made its ghostly visitations on every continent throughout recorded history. The Bookstore of Ashurbanipal haunts the earth until its soul, and the souls of the burnt books within, can be laid to rest.

Classics Books in Trenton, New Jersey, was a McGuffin Vortex, a place where the great sought-after objects of literature could finally be found. During its years in operation, customers located all sorts of objects hidden among the books: the jewel-encrusted falcon statue, the Fisher King's grail, Chekhov's gun (unfired), an everlasting gobstopper, the two horcruxes, a pair of silver shoes, the Infinity Stones, a pair of silver French candlesticks, a glass paperweight with pink coral inside, and a goose that laid golden eggs.

As great as these bookstores were, the greatest bookstore of all time was the Bookstore Al-jinn, located in the Abbasid Caliphate.

The Abbasid Caliphate was the third of the Islamic caliphates to succeed the prophet Muhammad. They ruled from Baghdad, the city that was a gift of God, the round city, the world's center of education and culture. For hundreds of years, Baghdad was home to the world's best astronomers, physicians, mathematicians, chemists, and poets. For example, the inventor of algebra lived there; his name was Al-Khawarizmi and he was the author of the book of math titled, *Katab al-Jabr*, from which algebra took its name. The city of Baghdad was a house of wisdom, and there was a school of learning there named just that.

In the middle of this flowering of wisdom and intelligence and beauty, on the edge of town, a bookstore appeared on the corner near a bakery and across from a potter. One day the corner was home to a mammoth kumta tree, with its rough blackish bark and its spiny branches. The next morning people in the neighborhood were surprised to find a bookstore selling books filled with all the knowledge and beauty of the greatest city in the world.

The proprietor, Abd Allah ibn Baḥr al-Kinānī al-Baṣrī, would not answer from whence he came. Or rather, he answered all the time, telling fanciful and contradictory stories. He came from Basra where he collected books and worked for a family of fishermen; he came from Cordoba where he studied languages and loved a forbidden woman and was forced to flee; he came from Damascus where he studied book-binding; he had been in Baghdad all along, but the neighbors were only now noticing him. When asked about the fanciful and perhaps fearful name of his store, he smiled a distant smile and said that was a joke he would share at another time.

No matter its origins, the Bookstore Al-jinn was quickly a favorite of Baghdad. Scientists and glassblowers, architects and laborers, students and travelers, all were welcome within the walls of the shop. It was a palace of books. Books were translated and transcribed. Books were read and purchased.

There was a back room, though, that few people were allowed to enter. It didn't matter if you were rich or powerful; with a glance, al-Basri would turn you away. But if you were innocent or heartbroken or world weary, he might let you in.

The back room was inexplicably as large as an ocean. The bookshelves reached into the sky. Lamps floated in the air and attendants wandered the room with plates of plums and pastries and wine for the book buyers there. As fantastic as it was, the room was ordinary and commonplace next to the books themselves.

They were unlike any books anywhere in the world. There were no histories or scientific tracts to be found. These books were filled with the fervent dreams of a better world. One section, with deep red carpets on the floor, was filled entirely of books of the prayers of children. Another, in tall, hand-carved bookcases, was filled with books of wishes made on dandelions and wishes made on coins thrown into wells and fountains. There were volumes of birthday wishes, wedding wishes and wishes made on shooting stars, wishes made on monkey paws and the broken bones of fowl.

In one corner, under lights made of green glass, were wishes made on the lamps of the djinn.

This was a library of hope, a bookstore of the dreams of a better world. Outside this bookshop, even in the most amazing city to ever exist—the pinnacle of wisdom and knowledge and beauty—even here, the world was cruel and indifferent, home to hunger, violence, misery, and the turning wheels of power and greed. The customers who visited the back room of the Bookstore Al-jinn could glimpse one of the seven heavens—the place where every prayer, wish and plea for a better world was collected and bound, a light in the cruel darkness of the world.

Baghdad was the best of all cities for 500 years, until the Mongols made the Tigris and Euphrates run red with the blood of scholars. For much of that time, Abd Allah ibn Baḥr al-Kinānī al-Baṣrī (under this first name and under subsequent aliases) maintained the corner bookstore and the back room of wishes. Then, as mysteriously as he appeared, he disappeared, leaving the mammoth kumta tree in its place.

Shoppers in used bookstores to this very day still get the feeling of magic and wonder, and the anticipation that somewhere in the stacks of their favorite bookshop, there is something waiting for them, an echo of the back room of the Bookstore Al-jinn, the sense of hope and possibility, and the wish for the betterment of an imperfect world.

The Last Bohemian of Avenue A (excerpt)

Yusef Komunyakaa

I bet you don't know why Duncan
plays up-tempo always, some glow
in the bell, some jive in the know?
Well, if you played a shiny bugle
in an army band for four years
blowing only reveille & taps,
you'd also second line on trumpet
till a gravedigger's soul came home
to roost on a broken weathervane.

You know, old boy, I gotta
drive up one of these days
& pay Sonny my respects.
They say he's beginning to pull
back, just a tad, to humble the
old cowhand days of burning
leather in the saddle. But I bet
he can brown any youngblood's
goose in a close cut at sunset.

I tell you, if I placed an LP
of his on a needle machine,
I'm afraid I may never again
open a door in the all-seeing
dark. Anyway, these days,
they don't pick up quarters
or teeth from the sidewalk.

I know to put my shoulder
to the eternal rally-wheel
grinding sweat into tunes.
Hard work I know, muscle
of give, ready to crank up
grab & hold, or to set free
the monster hiding inside.
All the great roll calls begin
in paradise & ends in hell,
& they know how Beauty
labors in the underworld.

The Last Bohemian of Avenue A (excerpt)

Work taught my muscles
to be gentle as the blues
grappling with a night
swollen with cicadas
& a pleading in the dark
along a river that never
takes no for benediction.
Sometimes, you must punch yes
up into a song, or wheels run off
the sad red wagon hauling dogwood.

Benny once took a photograph
from a notebook of drawings
of nine siblings lined up against
a Georgia sky, a dusky quietude
in their gaze. I remember him holding
the image this way & that way, up
to hard silence, as if he could see
into something. This was a week
or so after Raymond had shot
himself. I had to tear the photo
outta my friend's brotherly grip.

Can one face the beast with art
& expect to win freedom? Well,
if I knew the answer to the light
crawling from a dungeon or cave,
maybe my horns would have dust
in their bells, & when I say work
I always mean play. I keep
saying to a brother I never had,
Sonny, talk to me. You see,
when I said this I couldn't
help but think of Jimmy,
how I love that story.

Last Saturday I went home
an hour or two before my gig
at Candlelight, & when I stepped
into Classics the old country
whispered into my ears. I love
to finger pages, reading marginalia
& weighing the heft in my hands.
Lower East Side bookstores
are now gutted temples,
& when windows of St. Marks
were papered I felt the hurt.

But standing there in Classics,

leafing the pages, I felt at home.

my mind saying, *Killers of the Dream,*

& here's Jimmy's *Giovanni's Room.*

You know, once he said he threw

a glass of ice water at a mirror

in the American Diner, & something

in his tone—now a feeling inside me—

fretted an old call & response, saying,

The waitress was Eastern European

& this drove Jimmy off to Paris.

Three Tests for Evaluating a First Date

Eric Maywar

They argued about time travel for the entire 15-minute drive. Cole argued that time travel would have to be consistent because the universe is fixed. Somebody could travel back in time to attempt to change something only to find that their time travel had already happened and was essential to things turning out the way they did—like in *Terminator 1* or *Harry Potter*. He also argued that time travel would only happen through the application of physics. Samantha argued that time travel could change the past like *Back to the Future* or *Hot Tub Time Machine*. She also argued that time travel would happen through mental discipline, not physics, that a person could train herself, through sheer force of will, to travel through time. Cole said that was ridiculous, but whatever. The only thing they agreed on is that a time traveler should avoid meeting his or her former self; nothing good could come of that.

Samantha was enjoying arguing with Cole. It was part of the first-date test and he was passing. Would Cole lose his temper during a stupid argument? Would he be condescending and mansplain everything? Or would he listen to what she had to say no matter how ridiculous it was?

The second test was about bookstores, which is why they were driving from campus to Classics Books. Samantha had a theory that if she took a first date to a bookstore, she would know if he was worth a second date. Watching how men reacted to books was a good barometer. Were they intimidated? Did they enjoy books? Did their conversation keep drifting to football and video games even when surrounded by a bookstore?

She once dated a guy from New York who, when they met at a bar, told her that he owned a first edition of *The Lorax* (though he kept calling it *The Lomax*). Then, before she arrived at his apartment on the second date, he had purchased a copy on-line, so he could show off. Men, the ones worth avoiding, could be weird around books.

As first date material, Cole was doing alright, though he was a little full of himself. But maybe that was confidence? He walked slowly down the fiction aisle pointing to every book he had read and in what format he had read it. "Kindle. Kindle. Paperback. Kindle. Hardcover. Kindle."

Samantha said, playfully, "I can't stand Kindles. They don't feel right."

"It's the future. Don't fight it," he said.

"Books will always be here," she said. "When they invented escalators, stairs didn't go away. They both have their purpose. Isn't that right?" she said to an elderly man who was obviously eavesdropping on their conversation.

"That's right," the man answered. "These books, here, they exist. They aren't just some Word file to be lost in the Internet."

The man kept talking while Samantha smiled. "That's right. See, he agrees with me. Soon, you'll learn, you'll need to agree with everything I say as well."

Samantha was starting to get that feeling about Cole. Sure, he was a touch overbearing, but he was smart, and funny, and liked books. She got that sense of vertigo like she was on the edge of a cliff ready to fall.

Her eye caught her favorite book on one of the shelves, *The House on Mango Street*. Wonderful book, simple, lyrical, but laced with hidden danger. Every time she saw the book on a shelf, a warmth of emotions flooded over her—another power real books had over e-books.

She pulled the book from the shelf, idly. There was a paper inside. Samantha enjoyed finding ephemera in books. In bookstores past, she had found a four-leaf clover, a twenty-dollar bill in a six-dollar book, and love letters. She had found a ten-thousand-dollar check in a book, but it was a book on witchcraft, so she figured she would leave that check untouched. So, it is no surprise that she opened her favorite book to see what was on the paper. Anybody who knew her would have guessed she would do that.

The paper said:

The Third Test of a First Date

If your future self has figured out how to will herself through time and travels back to tell you to not go on a second date with Cole, always listen to her.

Love
Sam

Samantha froze for a moment, stunned, staring at the letter.

"What is it," asked Cole. "What's wrong?"

"Nothing," said Samantha slowly. "I've always loved this book…and I guess I always will."

At Classics Books

Doc Long

Old bookstores *Wise silence
*The overfed cat napping on the windowsill *

Specks of dust ride lasers of light
Stillness haunted in an unseen world

Open any book and the sulk of wine and incense
all the way from Dakar or Tashkent*

Subversive revolutionary* Things hidden
in the name of freedom * Music* Is that music*

Bebop walking down the street dancing reading
a book* The cat yawns goes back to sleep *

Small town *Saturday afternoon*
Planets swarming in silver light*

The Cat in the Hat in the Box in the Bookstore: A True Story

Eric Maywar

When I first opened the bookstore, I was adamant that it was going to be a store for readers, not collectors. I was not going to sell first editions; I was going to sell books for people who liked to read not collect; blah blah blah. Then somebody brought in a first edition of *War of the Worlds*. How cool it was to hold that book in my hands. It took me about 30 seconds to throw out my rule and carry some collectable books.

One busy Saturday at our first store, I had a line at the register and a woman came in with a box of books to donate. I invited her to wait a moment and I would let her know how much credit I could give her, but she said not to worry about it—she had just tried to sell these books at a garage sale and she just wanted to get rid of them. On the side of the box read "Old Kids Books $1 Each."

About a week later, one of the New Hope floods came and I had to pack up every book in the store. Martines (a restaurant across the street) let me pile up books on her tables (I would eat at a restaurant like that!), friends and customers loaded up their vans and cars and we emptied the store.

We already had Classics, a second used bookstore in Trenton, and we decided to close the New Hope store and deliver all the books to Trenton. We still hadn't opened that box of kids' books.

It took us months to settle in to the Trenton store, unpacking, sorting and shelving all the books from New Hope. It was maybe six months later that I opened the box of books.

It included a first edition early Maurice Sendak's *A Hole is to Dig* ($150) and a first edition Tasha Tudor ($800). But the mind-blowing book was a first edition (200/200 on the price tab of the flap) of *The Cat in the Hat.* It was in perfect condition, no single mark or scuff, no price clip. It looked unread. List price? $7,000. (We eventually sold it wholesale to another bookstore for about $2,000).

What an amazing collection of books, which had sat unwanted in a box at a garage sale for $1.

There is something essentially human about used books. Life may leave us a little battered and worn, but we still have the capacity to inspire, to teach, to entertain, to love and be loved.

And no matter how unwanted we may feel at times, how neglected and overlooked, all it takes is the right person to open our covers and recognize us for the treasure we are.

Elmore

Jeff Edelstein

The old man wasn't moving. That much was clear. He had parked himself on one of those step stools everyone uses as regular stools, and he was reading. Reading! In a bookstore.

I walked into Classics a bit past noon, and he was there.

I chatted with Eric, and he was still there.

I browsed through science fiction, ignoring fantasy, and yep, still there.

Checked out the thrillers. He hasn't moved.

"Get up," is what I wanted to say to him, but come on: I wasn't going to do that. I was simply going to have to stand directly behind him and hover over his old-man smelling sweater and sport coat combo if I wanted to browse the top shelf of the mystery section where the Elmore Leonard novels were housed. (Do we have time for an aside? Good. Of course Leonard belongs in the mystery section. He has always been in the mystery section. Except his books aren't really mysteries. They're yarns. There should really be a "Yarns" section in every bookstore. Anyway....)

Anyway, you should know this: I've read every Elmore Leonard book ever published, some of them twice, many of them three times. To call him "my favorite" author doesn't really do justice to my connection with the since-deceased scribe. It's...somehow more. I don't know how to put it into words. I feel like I know him. Knew him. I don't know. I'm just jibber-jabbering now, but if you've ever had a connection with an author like this, you know what I mean. It's cosmic. It's like we were conjoined at spiritual birth.

Yeah. That's it. Me and Elmore: Conjoined at spiritual birth.

I remember the first book I read by him: *Glitz*. I was 14 years old or so. I picked it out because A) my mother insisted I start reading other books besides sports books, and B) the cover looked cool.

I read most of it during a family vacation to Wildwood. The fact much of the action took place in Atlantic City thrilled me.

To be fair, much of the action went over my teenage head, but I loved it. Loved every minute of it.

Went back to the bookstore and started devouring, one by one, his oeuvre.

And so yeah: I've read 'em all. Every last one of them.

So why was I insistent on getting this old fart out of the way? Because I collect. Oh yes, I collect Elmore.

Doesn't matter if I read them all, my goal is to possess as many copies of different editions as I can. Hardcover, of course, but paperbacks as well. Some of his paperbacks have seven, eight, sometimes even 10 different covers.

I covet them all. I am always on the lookout.

And finding one of the old originals, from the 1970s, with the paper browned and the cover crinkly and the musty paperback smell—is there a better smell on Earth? I daresay not—well… that's a little slice of heaven for this guy.

And thus all I wanted to do in the 20 minutes or so I had during my lunch break was to thumb through the few dozen editions, that were sitting on the top shelf, and that were, quite literally, out of my reach due to this old asshat sitting down on a step stool and reading. Reading!

I caught a glimpse of what he was reading. *The Friends of Eddie Coyle* by George V. Higgins. A classic of the genre. A book Leonard himself was fond of.

This softened me a bit to the bespectacled geezer.

A bit.

But still.

It was 12:15. I needed my Elmore fix. I had about five minutes before I had to head back to the office.

Maybe a little subtle hint…

"Hey Eric!" I yelled from about two feet away from Old Man Who Sits. "You get any new Elmore stuff since I've been here last?"

I mean, the guy was reading Higgins. He had to know of Leonard. Maybe this would cause the guy to glance in my direction, maybe say, "Oh pardon me young man, was I in your way? Please, allow me to shuffle off to my certain death so you can…"

"I think so," Eric yelled back. "Take a look."

I stood there staring at the old man.

Nothing.

He just licked his thumb and turned the next page.

My blood pressure ticked up a few notches.

It wasn't happening. The guy wasn't moving. What a disaster and then…

He stood up.

Well, he started to stand up.

It took an eternity.

I was like a dog seeing his master through the screen door. The excitement was too much. Just move…just move…just move… and…

He moved enough so that I could kick the step stool out of the way and get my grimy hands on a little bit of Elmore.

He left behind a trail of stale cigarette smell. Gross. Didn't matter, though. On to the task at hand!

I looked at the spines of the books, keeping a running tally in my head … "that's an '88 *Bandits*, have that, the original '76 *Swag*, have that, all these recent ones I've got…"

This went on for about 45 seconds. I had them all. No new treasures for me today. What a waste.

Still had a few minutes before I had to get back to the office.

I crouched down to the bottom of the shelf on the left of Elmore and picked up the *Friends of Eddie Coyle* the old man was reading.

I pulled the step stool back and sat down. I yanked the book open to a random page, just to get a taste.

I heard the door to the store open with the familiar jangle of the bells.

"See you again, Eric," I heard someone say in an old-man voice, probably the Old Man himself.

"Take it easy, Dutch," Eric replied.

What the Bookseller Knew

Eric Maywar

ONE. While bookstores share a general, bookish smell, each is distinctive, like the differences in coffee or Scotch. Each bookstore has its own special blend: the ratio of fresh inkiness of books just published to the browning pulp of vintage paperbacks, maybe a cat, maybe coffee, maybe overtones of the smokehouse from up the street or the perfume of a customer who had lingered there during lunch.

TWO. Bookstores are sensual. Book people are great lovers. These people are happy to take their time with something they love; they feel no need to rush. They will spend hours in bed with no regret. They are sensualists. They enjoy the weight of a book in their hands, the texture of the spine, the smell of its pages.

THREE. Used bookstores are places that bring out the best in people (the way the DMV brings out the worst): the meanest, most shallow man in the world enters a used bookstore and is illuminated from within by that one book, that one idea, that one beautiful phrase that makes him his better self.

FOUR. Used bookstores are havens for readers in an unkind world. Collectors of first editions and school children on their way home, solitary readers and book-club members, closeted poets and argumentative intellectuals: they all find a home in the cozy clutter of a true used bookstore, a shelter from whatever troubles, real and imagined, that wait for them when they leave the shop.

Searching for Adventure

Nancy Scott

I left my six smart-ass kids at home
and walked the streets of Krakow
searching for lost relatives,
roamed bustling souks of Cairo,
blew up a house and escaped
from a burning car in Trenton.
Nerves frazzled, I sipped a cup
of bush tea in Botswana,
where I learned secrets
of a ladies' detective agency,
trekked Saharan sands
with a madman who promised me
safe passage to Dakar.
Came home to the daily slog,
dirty dishes, mutt thick with fleas,
hubby glued to Nascar.
Who needs this? I'm heading back
to Classics Bookstore
in search of more adventures.

Consider This

Doc Long

Cross country in California

Cross latitudes and longitudes

The attitudes vicissitudes

A long way from Classic Books in downtown Trenton

A twenty-two year old man was shot dead seven times

Shot into infinity oblivion

Seven times into eternity

He was in his grandmother's backyard

Planting flowers praying dreaming

Maybe talking to himself about himself

About doing better

Boom seven times

Seven angels seven trumpets seven divine things

Police say they thought his cell phone was a weapon

Although no books or gun was found at the scene

Records show the young man's mind and soul

Were thousands of years old

Imagine that

And that such things have been happening

More frequently for a very long time

If you want to you can look it up

Find the names of all the dead listed in certain books

Books Loved and Worthy and Solid Like a Whisky Glass

Eric Maywar

The old man walked down Warren Street smelling the warm cakes from L'TEC and the brisket from the Smokehouse. He stopped for a moment on the corner of Warren and Lafayette, listening to the music coming from Yusef's Place, jazz the way it was meant to be heard, live in the moment in an intimate space, the three musicians calling and responding, bound together by the music they made, about as close as three people could be. Then the song ended and the old man moved on.

Around the corner on Lafayette Street, the bookstore was open. The light from the windows spilled onto the sidewalk.

Wind chimes set against the door sounded as he pushed his way inside. Books were stacked shoulder high on both sides of the door, at times neatly arranged and carefully chosen; other times, scattered.

The bookseller nodded and said something friendly, then went back to the stack of books in front of him. That is the way a bookstore should be, the old man thought. They've gone to the trouble to create a universe of books, curated and shelved for the old man's pleasure, and were smart enough to not interrupt his browsing.

Deep in the fiction section, the old man carefully selected two books: *The Magus* by John Fowles and *The Unbearable Lightness of Being* by Milan Kundera. He had read them both, years earlier, and remembered loving them. Shouldn't you return to the books that you once loved?

He also bought a book of photography. On the cover was a picture of a blur of a boy standing on top of a speeding train, as if he were surfing, his deep brown eyes staring right at the camera the moment the photograph was shot.

The old man liked that used bookstores let you be. For him, it was a better place than a bar or a restaurant. There was no minimum number of drinks to purchase and no hurry to leave a table so more customers could sit. You could exist at your own pace in a bookstore. There was good conversation if he wanted it, but he found as he got older he liked listening to other conversations more than he liked talking. Listening, he could be alone, but also not alone, at the same time.

At the end of the aisle, two college students were pointing to books on shelves that they had read, ostensibly to share but mostly to show off.

The man was pointing to the spines of trade paperbacks, reciting the format in which he read the book. "Kindle. Kindle. Paperback. Kindle. Hardcover. Kindle."

The woman pouted a face. "I can't stand Kindles. They don't feel right."

The old man knew that the woman was a book person. Book people understood there was something sacred in a used bookstore. Books weren't just paper versions of e-books. Books were totemic. Their physicality meant something.

The woman felt the connection too; she had caught something in the old man's eye. "Books will always be here," she said. "When they invented escalators, stairs didn't go away. Isn't that right?" she said to the old man.

"That's right," he answered slowly. "These books, here, they exist. They aren't just some Word file to be lost in the Internet.

Used books show care—the care of the author, sure, and the publisher, but also the care of the binder who created them, the care of the bookstore owner who arranged them for consideration, the care of its first owner and all the subsequent owners who handled this particular copy and read it and loved it. Books are loved and worthy and solid like a whisky glass. Or a heart."

The old man stopped talking. He had realized he wasn't talking about books any more. He felt a touch of embarrassment until the woman said to the man, "That's right. See, he agrees with me." She hadn't understood what he was saying, just as he had barely understood while he was saying it.

Like the books surrounding the old man, his life had showed care, the care of his family, the care of every friend who chose him, though he was at an age where few of those friends were still around. He showed the care of his first wife who eventually left him when they grew into the people they were meant to be. He showed the care of his second wife who had died before he did. Like the used books around him, he had a history and he was not worth any less just because he was no longer new, that he had been cared for several times over. Maybe the old man felt a kinship with the books who were on shelves with many others but essentially alone, just like the people in the bookstore. This woman, this man, the bookstore owner, the jazz musicians and the boy in the book on the top of the train each have their own story, for the most part unknown to one another, sitting cover to cover, yet miles apart.

The old man paid for his books and left the bookstore, to the farewell tinkling of wind chimes, exiting onto Lafayette Street. He paused for a moment by himself under the gooseneck lights of the shop and then disappeared alone into the night.

Certain Queer Times and Occasions: An Exercise in Ridiculousness

David Lee White

CHARACTERS
ERIC—Owns a bookstore
WYATT—A gentleman from New York

SCENE—Classics Books, Trenton, NJ

AT RISE—ERIC is in Classics Books

(WYATT enters)

WYATT
Well, well, well. What have we here? What a delightful, charming little place you have.

ERIC
Thank you.

WYATT
There are books here!

ERIC
Yes. It's a bookstore.

WYATT

A bookstore! We have those in New York. That's where I live.

ERIC

Ah. Welcome to Trenton. I'm Eric.

WYATT

Thank you. Quaint city you have here. I seldom leave the island of Manhattan, but I had business at the capital this weekend. I'm staying at the hotel across the way.

ERIC

The hotel is closed. It's been closed for ages.

WYATT

Really? Well that explains why the shower is cold and I can never get room service. Ha! In any case, I thought I'd take a wander around your adorable little downtown and I have to say, this is a delightful store you have here. You, sir, are a real credit to your city.

ERIC

Uh...thanks.

WYATT

Not much competition though, is there? In New York, we have hundreds of bookstores. Practically one on every corner. Sometimes two per corner. By God, it's a city of bookstores!

ERIC

Yes, I've been there. I've been to the Strand a few times.

WYATT

The Strand? Ha! That's for tourists! We also have secret book-
stores that only New Yorkers know about! Some of them are
hundreds of feet underground! I know of one store that only sells
Hemingway first editions! Would you like to go there?

ERIC

Uh…sure.

WYATT

You can't! It's only for New Yorkers! You have to know the secret
knock!

ERIC

Gotcha. Say, I'm only open until 2:00 and it's 1:50 now–

WYATT

I am in search of a volume!

ERIC

Oh. Okay. What is it? We've got a lot of stuff here.

WYATT

I doubt you have this book. It's quite rare. If I could only think of
the title. Let's see…it's about an archaeologist. And he discovers
that the secret of Jesus Christ's lineage is hidden in the works of
Leonardo da Vinci.

ERIC

The Da Vinci Code.

WYATT

What?

ERIC

The book is called *The Da Vinci Code.*

WYATT

No, that's not it.

ERIC

Sure it is.

WYATT

No, no. And there's this cult called Opus Dei and they protect
the secret and whip themselves and they're kind of Catholic but
not really.

ERIC

I am sure that's *The Da Vinci Code.*

WYATT

No, you're thinking of the wrong book. The one I'm thinking
of was made into a movie with Tom Hanks and an adorable
French actress.

ERIC

So help me God, it's *The Da Vinci Code.* I have three copies.

(ERIC finds a copy of *The Da Vinci Code.*)

ERIC

Look. (opening the book) Opus Dei. Archaeology. It's *Da Vinci
Code.*

WYATT

Don't be absurd. I've never seen this book before and wouldn't read it anyway. I would never read something that uses such a common font!

ERIC

Okayyyyy…

WYATT

Obviously, you don't have what I'm looking for.

ERIC

Well it was nice meeting you.

WYATT

Perhaps you have another volume on my search list!

ERIC

Oh, God.

WYATT

It's obscenely rare. Only a handful of copies were ever printed. Chilling little tale about a teenage girl who gains psychic powers and takes revenge on the high school students that torment her.

ERIC

It's called *Carrie.*

WYATT

No. And then they pour pig blood on her and she kills everyone at prom.

ERIC

Carrie. It's by Stephen King. The book is called *Carrie.*

WYATT

Her mother prays all the time and everyone laughs at her when she gets her period.

ERIC

Stop it.

WYATT

Clearly you don't have it. Do you have anything?

ERIC

There are thousands of books here. And we have *Carrie.* We probably have every Dan Brown and Stephen King novel as well as hundreds and hundreds and hundreds of books. We have antiquarian books. We have pulp novels. We have books on religion. We have science-fiction. We have an African-American section. True Crime. Children's books. Cookbooks. Shakespeare. Signed editions. First editions.

WYATT

How about *Moby Dick?*

ERIC

I have *Moby Dick!*

(ERIC runs to a shelf.)

WYATT

Have you even heard of *Moby Dick?*

ERIC

I have two copies! Would you like it abridged or unabridged?

WYATT

It's about a man hunting a shark!

ERIC

Whale. He's hunting a whale.

WYATT

And his name is Ishmael!

ERIC

It's Ahab!

WYATT

And the three shark hunters get in a small boat and go searching for the killer shark!

ERIC

That's *Jaws*. It's not the same as *Moby Dick!* You're thinking of *Jaws*. It was published in 1974 and made into a movie.

WYATT

Moby Dick would make a horrible movie.

ERIC

Literally everyone in the world knows the difference between *Moby Dick* and *Jaws*.

WYATT

If this were New York, I could walk twenty feet, knock on an unmarked door and be ushered into a secret bookstore where they would answer my questions and fetch me a copy of *Moby Dick!*

ERIC

Well this is Trenton! Get out of my store!

WYATT

What? How dare you! Is this how the capital city of New Jersey treats people? I see! Well, fear not! I will never cross your threshold again! Good day, sir!

(WYATT exits the store. We hear the sound of a car backfiring. ERIC runs to the window and looks out. We hear a high-pitched shriek. The door opens and WYATT re-enters, holding his leg.)

WYATT

Help! I've been shot!

ERIC

That was just a car backfiring.

WYATT

Nonsense! I've been struck in the leg by a bullet!

ERIC

I saw the car. It wasn't a gun.

WYATT

I think I know what a bullet in the leg feels like! I live in New York!

ERIC

It was a car. It was just a car and I hate you.

WYATT

Please just let me die in peace. Oh, to think I'll never see home again. If only I was on 95 South heading back to New York.

ERIC

95 South goes into Philadelphia. Are you from Philadelphia?

WYATT

I don't know. I might be delirious. Maybe I'm from Baltimore. Where's the Liberty Bell?

ERIC

Philadelphia.

WYATT

Oh, what do you know?

ERIC

If you really think you're hurt, I'll call an ambulance.

WYATT

You're so kind. Perhaps I was too hasty in my judgement. Too prideful. Too arrogant. We're like that in Baltimore.

ERIC (into phone)

Yeah, I've got someone in my store that's been hurt. Classics on Warren and Lafayette.

WYATT

My point is, I'm sorry. I should never have criticized your fair city. It's quite nice here in Hamilton.

ERIC

We're in Trenton. (into phone) I know you know! Yes, I'll see you soon. (hangs up the phone) The ambulance will be here shortly.

WYATT

Thank you. Read to me while we wait, will you?

ERIC

Read to you?

WYATT

From *Moby Dick*. Please, Aaron.

ERIC

Eric.

WYATT

Please read.

(ERIC sighs and sits down on the floor. He picks up a copy of *Moby Dick* and begins reading.)

ERIC

"There are certain queer times and occasions in this strange mixed affair we call life when a man takes this whole universe for a vast practical joke, though the wit thereof he but dimly discerns, and more than suspects that the joke is at nobody's expense but his own. Ahab sighed. Seconds later, the killer shark struck the hull. 'We need a bigger boat,' said Ahab."
(ERIC sits stunned, looks at the cover of the book, then back at the pages. The color drains from his face.)

END OF PLAY

Anything You Need

Ilene Dube

I boarded the express in Brooklyn that morning.

"This train is making no local stops," announced the conductor, the brass buttons on his epaulets shining like gold. Outside the window, I viewed the seamless transition from one set of industrial-era buildings to another—the gray skies soon had me craving a coffee.

The rush of passengers in wool and down swept me onto a concrete platform where a passing train created a gust of wind that would have blown my wig, had I been wearing one.

I passed a park and then went through another, and a few blocks down found myself entering a bookshop. The tinkling of the door chimes drowned the sounds of outside, transporting me to another world. The purveyor, a man with a beard and a button-down shirt, looked up. "Let me know if there's anything you're looking for."

"Coffee?" I knew the answer before the word escaped.

He told me about a nice place on Cass Street, but it was too far to walk on this blustery day. He showed me a selection of books on coffee, but their covers, with images of dark-roasted beans and laurel leaf patterns in milk foam only deepened my cravings.

The store was filled with blond wood shelves packed with books. There were only single copies of each title. Books were also piled onto tables and in boxes. The smell of old books was like a mix of chocolate and—oh god—coffee.

There were cookbooks and art books, and books I'd read years ago: *The Master and Margarita, One Hundred Years of Solitude, Things Fall Apart, One Flew Over the Cuckoo's Nest, Beloved, Slaughterhouse Five.*

"I'm looking for my great grandfather," I told the proprietor. "He was an ironworker. His son, my grandfather, grew up on a cooperative farm for Jewish immigrants in New Jersey. His brother became a butcher in Trenton. He was murdered in his shop. His son was an architect who worked with Louis Kahn on the Trenton Bath House."

I'm not sure how much of what I said was true. That is, I'd known these things to be true before boarding the train that morning, but as I spoke these truths I began to wonder.

The proprietor led me to a section on Trenton history. *Crossroads of the American Revolution* went too far back in time. *Trenton: Images of America* focused on landmark buildings. Where were the Dubes of Trenton?

"You might try the Trenton Free Public Library," the pleasant store owner suggested. "Or the State Archives."

I wondered if either of those places had coffee.

I was now aware of a group gathered at the back of the store. Mostly women, they were knitting. Or talking about knitting. Or laughing about knitting.

One of the women came to the front. Balancing with a cane, she walked slowly. "Did you want to know about the butcher who was murdered?" she asked.

I nodded. "Louis Dube."

"I used to go there for meat," she said, her face suddenly becoming young again. "Lou was my mother's butcher. Everyone in Trenton was devastated by what happened."

As it turns out, there'd been a reading the previous week by the author of a book about Trenton in the 1930s. The talk was so well received; the book had not only sold out but was out of print. But it may have had a footnote about Louis the murdered butcher.

The old woman introduced me to the knitting group. They greeted me like a long-lost relation. I confessed I didn't know how to knit. One woman handed me a kit. It was for a blanket that had different panels outlining my family history, from the ironworker who left Russia to the cooperative farming communities and the murder at the butcher shop.

A woman with curly hair that matched the yarn she was using opened the plastic wrapper, took out the needles and cast on stitches in a golden thread. Then she handed the needles to me, and soon I was knitting for the first time in my life. Every stitch, seemingly made at lightning speed, was perfectly neat.

We heard the tinkling of the door chimes. The coffee vendor had arrived! He had bicycled over with his coffee cart. "Trenton Makes Coffee," read his shirt. He even smelled like coffee as he made us each a cup of the best brew I'd ever had. In the crema on top, I could see my grandfather's beard. It curled like the yarn of the woman who'd taught me to knit.

The proprietor called me to the front of the store. He'd remembered something: "Sasha Parubchenko—Trenton's blacksmith. Maybe he can tell you something."

The bicycling coffee roaster was waiting for me outside. As I climbed aboard the back of his bike, the woman with the sheepskin hair came running after me, presenting the knitted blanket of my family history. I wore it on my back like a cape as suddenly the coffee roaster's bicycle lifted off the ground. Below, I could see the crowd at Classics Books, waving at us in the sky.

The Bookshop on Lafayette Street

The Bookseller and the Troll

Eric Maywar

The bookseller knew there was something happening in the rare book section when there was a shattering of glass and a terrible roar that turned into a deep-throated cackle. When the troll rounded the corner and fixed the bookseller with his haggard and malevolent eye, the bookseller knew he was going to have to stop pricing books.

"I have been trapped in that book by that witch's curse for 600 years," bellowed the troll. "My belly is six hundred years empty. I plan to break my fast with a seller of books."

The troll stood nine feet tall and had to stoop to fit under the ceiling of the bookstore. His hair was a shaggy lion's mane. His nails and teeth were yellow and sharp. He smelled like leather and halitosis.

The bookseller stood six feet tall and was wearing a tee shirt that read, "If you think reading is boring, you are doing it wrong." He put down the book he was pricing and looked at the troll.

"What's next? Usually at this point in the story, there is some riddle I need to solve or task I need to perform. Do I need to guess your name? Trick you into shape-changing into a fly?"

The troll threw his head back and laughed a horrible laugh. "You are doomed, man of books. You have one chance, and it is an impossible task. To return me to the book in which I was trapped for 600 years, you must perform a Herculean feat. You must tell me what book I came out of! There is no way you can possibly guess. You need to guess one of the 20,000 books that you have in this store!"

"Do I get three guesses?"

The troll laughed again. "No, puny man of books. This is no child's fairy tale. You get one guess. Then I will eat you up!"

The bookseller turned to his computer. He opened the database with the inventory of all the books in the rare book cases. Then he went to Google and typed in "fairy tales troll."

"I don't know what you think you are doing with that puny box and that click click clacking. Nothing can help you now!" said the troll, looking over the bookseller's shoulder. "And what is a goggle?"

"I hope magic doesn't hold pronunciation against me. You came from the Prose Edda book *Skáldskaparmál*," said the bookseller.

"Noooooo!" howled the troll as he was sucked back into the book that was his prison, which had fallen on the floor in the rare books section. "How could you know the answer to that question? It was impossible!"

The bookstore fell quiet. The bookseller looked over at the broken glass from the rare books shelf and the books that the troll had knocked over and slowly got up to get a broom.

Service Call

Tom Webster

It's all about the service calls. Ok, ok: installation is about contractors and construction. I know where that leads. Everybody wants some, right? You can pad the hours like there's no tomorrow and no one will say anything because they're all doing it too. But the service call, the repair, is feeding the monkey. And these days, you don't have to wait for them to call.

Eric, the manager of the bookstore, didn't look especially surprised when I walked through the door. The building was older than he—and he was pushing late eighties—and I had been sticking sensors all over the goddamn place. They pick up the slightest bit of moisture and send a signal to a slightly larger unit I hardwired in by the circuit box. The extra time I spent making it to level-five service tech was worth it, because I can do damn near anything. I'm mostly into plumbing systems, but I can do electric, HVAC, rough carpentry, general troubleshooting, inspections, and appraisals. I don't like doing anything that requires a great deal of human interaction, or talking at all, really, though, so those last two are pretty much reserved for friends. Eric is a pretty good guy, but maybe a little too weird to be a friend. Not special weird, like my daughter. Just fucked up in a generally agreeable way. Old man.

So this service call is about a sensor behind the bathroom. Lavatory sink, drain system, moisture. Back in the day—and I get to say that, pushing fifty-five—that would have been a nightmare. Mismatched piping, shit like that. To some degree, it still is. I mean, just because I get new gizmos every day doesn't mean I have to use them. I'm cobbling new stuff onto old, and that can be a pain in the ass. Still, I keep Eric's place (well, it's not his place. He just runs it. If anything, the bookstore owns him. Who isn't owned by someone or something else? Who has a place of his own? I don't have a place, really. I get the call from a sensor. I follow up on it. Neither Eric nor I think a lot about it. He sells books, or whatever. I fix shit. Anyway—) running for him.

I have to really get down in a low gap behind the wall to work on the line, and that sucks—like I said, I'm pushing fifty-five, and I don't do yoga—but the fix is easy. Old copper and a little PEX. What possessed me to leave that behind? I remove the section, using the same twist cutter my dad used, and I replace a long section with soft plastic. The pieces have a fair amount of give, like the PEX (honestly, it's just better PEX), so I can be pretty sloppy cutting them if I want, but I hate that, so I take my time. I spray it, briefly, to set it, and then I stick on another sensor and tap it with my watch. My watch knows where I am—always—so it puts the sensor in some data bank and runs the whole repair down. I add a photo, which is hard to take, lying on my back. Of course, it's hot as hell in there, between the walls, but that's the job. A little sweat, a little work. Better than yoga. And it kills the time.

I have a lot of time. Everyone has a lot of time. Right? So I fill it. Thirty years ago, I had a crapload of paperwork to deal with after every job. Now, it's nothing, really: snap one off and roll. I packed my gear and headed out past Eric, who held a book out to me. I took it without thinking, and walked through the door.

I turned over the book in my hands as the van drove me to the next job. I used to look at the map—hell, I used to drive, call the customer, all that crap—but I suppose the years get to us all, eventually. It didn't matter, really, where I was going. It didn't matter, really, what I had to do. I always followed the prompt.

The book cover looked pretty boring, until I flipped it over and realized it was one of those Manga things. When I was a kid, the school kept telling me to read: read, kid, they said, and you'll be successful. Of course, all the stuff I read was the same synthesized nonsense, about the chosen ones, the cast-off products of divine romance, or brave survivors. That shit made me fall asleep. Our school had a contest: who can read the most sleep-inducing shit? Not me. I winged it into the back, which, theoretically, should have stopped the van, but quality control being what it is, our journey continued, unhampered by such things as safety devices. Half of my job was getting around that stuff, anyway. Sometimes, it was about code: sometimes, it was about patience. It was never about money.

Eric, for instance, gave me books. But it's not like he was really rewarding me. He was promoting, never fear. He never stopped. But what about his bill, you ask. My watch recorded the repair, right? What about it? He owes everybody money. I owe everybody money. Everyone I know owes everybody money. We all owe the goddamn bank. I go places, I get stuff, my watch takes note. I go to work, and my watch takes note. I follow the prompt. Can I buy things? Even nice things? I guess. Anyone can. It's all the same stuff. All the stuff of the TV: the same stuff.

The van pulled up at the next job, and the timer did its thing, tossing off the ticks to the dreaded last minute, when the flag would go up and the Word would come down from on High, yea and verily. I wasn't worried about it: I have seniority enough that my jobs never really went over. Sometimes I sweated a little, but it kept me on my toes. I used to get by on half the time. I'm not done yet. This time, I was working a house job. No water. The lady couldn't decide what to do with me. Clearly, I had a job, but I was not a suit. She was a little embarrassed.

"I'm sure I paid the bill," she promised, about seventy-two times. I believed her. Everyone paid the bill. She was old, though, older than I. A kid wouldn't give a shit.

"I don't work for those people," I said. "I'm just contracted out." It was kind of true. Look: I was obviously working for the city of Trenton, but I am not a city employee. Some jackass in a tie listened to a voice mail and will watch my report later, then click off some numbers, then click off some more numbers, then someone will be happy. This way, the city apparently doesn't really need a water department because they have me. They still pay me, daily, and they pay a bunch of other people, so I don't actually know if they save any money. The hive-mind people—the bean counters—they all figure that stuff out, and argue about it online for all of us to watch, when we get bored with soap operas and football. But it's just another job to me. Follow the prompt.

I brought up the map of the outside lines on my watch, and used my high-tech tool—a shovel—to uncover a valve, which I cut out and replaced. The replacement wasn't especially different because this stuff is pretty much nineteenth century, and requires that kind of solution. I did throw on a couple sensors (function, not moisture) that would save Grandma the next phone call. If this thing failed again, someone would show up and fix it. Then, the jackass in a tie would click off some numbers, and the whole thing would be recorded, lost, ignored, or whatever.

The day's last job was funny—a young up-and-coming couple were certain they needed a new washing machine. Hell, they wanted to buy a new machine. Itching for it. They had pricey tans and goop in their hair. They were the kind of ding-dongs who talked about a house having "good bones" and how they could "open up the space." Up to their assholes in debt, like me, I guess. You gotta spend it on something. I buy dog treats for Cathy's service dog.

"Look," Captain Expensive Jacket (he was wearing it inside) said, "When I shut the door, it just stops. Do you think it's the pump? Or some computer thing? Is that repairable?" I could see what it was, but I dutifully peered at the machine for five painful minutes. I thought the lady was gonna chew her finger off. Eventually, I showed them that the latch was stuck, and that the safety system was cutting the power. Plastic issues. You can buy the nicest crap in the world, but it still comes down to bits of plastic.

"That's a relief," the good Captain said, sheepish. He had been surreptitiously looking at the newest model (in magenta) on his watch.

"Yeah," I agreed. "I've registered the call as 'instructional,' so it'll be cheaper." They didn't care; the money was just a number, after all. I get that.

The day ended as it frequently did: sitting at the bar, watching the Eagles on a foolish Monday night appearance against the Giants. My usual stool, Naugahyde and reconstituted plasti-wood, supported my sad ass as I sucked on a beer. Murphy, a regular who wore mismatching plaids and a deerstalker, shouted into my ear. Specials did that shit all the time. I stared at my beer.

"What kind of beer is that?" he demanded. Then: "This is Crabhammer! It's local! It's sour! Try some!" He pushed it at me. I didn't smile. I didn't frown. That's how you work with specials, you know. My daughter Cathy is a special. Holidays are a hoot. But if you encourage her, you're done with your evening. I nodded at him and looked at Nancy, the bartender.

"Murphy," she said, with the schoolteacher voice. Murphy looked at her, looked at me. Went back to his stool.

"Thanks," I said. It's not that I dislike Murphy, especially. But some nights I don't like a dissertation—which, as far as I can tell, is frequently fabricated—on whatever the hell Murphy is bent about. Of course, by law, I have to respect him as a person, and so on. You can't poke someone in the nose because they won't shut up. That's why I like drinking around people like Nancy. Anyway, I had no idea what beer I was drinking. I don't really care about that. I care about fixing things a certain way. That matters to me. I don't give all that much about what I eat and drink, as long as it doesn't kill me right away.

The Eagles began the long, slow, inevitable trudge toward oblivion, and I decided to join them. I waved at Nancy, nodded carefully but noncommittedly at Murphy, and went home. My watch paid my bill when I left, and, as Nancy was clocked in, my default tip for her (a little high, not too high) was added. I didn't even have to think about it, really. So I didn't.

While the van took me home, I straightened up the gear for the next day, and came across the book, which, as I said, was a Manga. A bald guy in a red cape punched furiously at the air. I stuck it in my pocket—Cathy might like it—and went into my apartment. The Eagles struggled back to life on the living room wall unit as I walked in, but I waved it off. Enough, I thought. Let this be the end.

Three days later, I had a sensor trip at the bookstore. My computer locked horns with Eric's—though that's really not very accurate; neither of us "has" or "owns" a computer—and scheduled a visit. Eric never had to be there, but he always was. He nodded at me, and I crawled into the wall. Another section of the old stuff needed replacement. I replaced a little more, bending the code a little, knowing that I might get a message from a distant suit when he saw the footage, but I was betting that he wouldn't give a shit—if I kept the numbers good, and I always did—he would waive it. And if he waived it, the next suit up the line was likely to waive it. It didn't save me time, but it didn't cost me time, either. That was key.

Eric had another book in his hand as I walked by. I took it. A bird guide.

"Eric," I said, "I almost never read these books." He smiled. Shrugged.

"You never know," he said. Then: "Earlier this year, a different guy came in to work on the plumbing." I nodded.

"Sure," I said. "I had some mandatory vacation time."

"Right," he said. "Mandatory." He chuckled. "Anyway," he went on, "this other guy came in to work on the system. And he wanted to change out all sorts of things—the heating, the plumbing, and so on. He pointed out that I could get grants to pay for all of it anyway, so why not? I put him off somehow. I don't remember how." He looked pointedly at the book in my hand. "You," he noted, "have never suggested anything like that."

"I recognize that shit changes," I said. "That doesn't mean I have to give in and roll around on my fucking back. Even if it's a good idea. Especially if it's a good idea." I found that my voice had risen.

Eric was full out laughing. "Who knows? We all get lucky from time to time."

"Sure," I said, pocketing the book and walking out the door. "You, me, and the Flying Dutchman."

A Fall Outing

Jackie Reinstedler

Driving up to the bookstore I checked my watch. Only 2 hours, 35 minutes left in my eleven-year-old's four hour leave from the boy's facility. Fall weather, the heartbreaking crush of red leaves, we opened the front door. Grandpa was along, still youthful with a bounce in his step, and gifted-smart.

My son wanted to learn about black holes, so he and Grandpa headed back to "science."

I stayed in the "thriller" and "mystery" sections, hoping a good story about an alcoholic detective who redeems himself would alter my reality.

* * *

Thirty-seven minutes later Grandpa and my son find me. Both hold a stack of books five books deep. The black holes book, a psychology book about dreams, and a book about ghosts in Alaska fill their arms. The other books weigh heavily, but are easily supported by my father and son.

The collection reflected my son's wonderful, curious, and brilliant mind. I had assumed this intelligence may inoculate him from the listless depression he had fallen into over the summer. Bullies or video games? Chemical or environmental? His father and I stood by until our son grew pale and disengaged. Scared, we found a boys' facility to treat our boy.

But now he was back, interested in the workings of the world again. Were his green eyes still guarded or absent? I was not sure. Already it was time to leave, to start the hour-long drive back to the boys' facility.

Grandpa and grandson waited for me at the check-out counter, but I wanted to stay in the bookstore. Classics was my oasis for now, a refuge, a shelter. It was time to leave the warmth of the bookstore and bring my son back.

Our books would sustain us for now.

Wise Silence

Doc Long

People pretend not to notice

The herd of elephants sleeping in the bookstore

And elephants never did do a lot of talking

Although they have read all of the books

Traveled around the world

Been into outer space and back

And know secrets about almost everything

They are cool and smart like that

Ask them any question you want

And if anyone accidently bumps into one of them

The elephants always say excuse me first

But most of the time no one hears them

Because they are so captivated

By all the amazing books and radical silence

Angel's Dram

Eric Maywar

Outside, wind-driven snow slapped into the dark, wet Trenton streets. A storm howled against the windows. Andrew Hanton stood just inside of the automatic doors and savored the immediate comfort of the hotel. The wintered city seemed suddenly distant in the warmth of the lobby. Andrew didn't stomp his feet or rub his hands together; he stood quietly, a wet paper bag in his gloved hands, letting the chill leave him slowly.

People with half-familiar faces wandered in and out of the main ballroom down the hall from the lobby. The National Marketing Research Organization was throwing their end-of-the-year party and laughter and music trailed out after stray members. Andrew thought they looked happy enough.

Andrew followed a carpet forward into an empty area, an upright Cherrywood Steinway piano standing in the corner. He set his damp paper bag on the floor, unbuttoned his jacket and folded his gloves into his pockets. Still invigorated by the brutal cold, he sat to enjoy the feeling.

The empty room was set like a corner pocket off the main lobby. The piano rested in the corner, chairs strategically arranged around small tables that would have held ashtrays thirty years ago. The room suggested Manny's or Cat Bones, dark smoky places a young Andrew would sneak in to play a set and get home before his dad sobered up. This room seemed disconnected from today, nostalgic and haunting. He liked it.

Andrew almost stood and went to the piano. He almost played "Wee Small Hours, "Waterfront," "Oriole."

Two other men walked over to him. They were both from

the party. The average man was Somebody Flood at Diagnostics Marketing in Philadelphia and the boy in the nice suit was Doug Something-that-sounds-like-Man-of-Cheviots. Andrew had taken a mnemonics course, but it never helped him remember a thing. He stood and smiled.

"Andrew, right?" asked Somebody Flood, shaking Andrew's hand.

"Yes, good to see you again. How are things in Philadelphia?"

"Good. Had a good quarter," Flood replied blandly.

Doug Man-of-Cheviots led with his business card. "Doug Onyshkevych. Rotorblade Tabulation and Analysis Software. How are you doing today?"

The three men sat. The wind shook the windows.

"What's in the bag?" asked Doug, pointing to Andrew's feet.

Andrew reached down and picked up his paper bag. He pulled out a bottle of Laphroaig Select, carefully folded the bag and set it under the bottle.

"Sick of free Champagne, I guess," said Flood. When he spoke, his sentences were short and incomplete, as if he were conserving energy.

Andrew smiled. "I need something a little more substantial. Something with a little smoke in it."

"Always liked a man who takes his drink seriously," said Flood.

"I was talking to the clerk when I bought this," said Andrew. "He told me something interesting. A whisky still has a life of about twenty years. When they put in a new still, they worry about the shape of the new still changing the taste. They go so far that if there was a dent in the old still, the distillery puts a dent in the new still in the same place. That way they hope the taste won't be changed. Now that's somebody who takes his drink seriously."

"I wonder if that's just superstition or if there's some truth to that."

Andrew shrugged. "Maybe a little of both. Every bottle of whisky is a little science and a little faith."

"I don't blame you one bit, stepping out for a bottle," said Flood. "I am bored to tears in there. I have a good book in my room from the bookstore across the street and that suits me just fine."

Flood caught Andrew looking at the piano. "Do you play?" he asked.

"I used to. In clubs, sort of."

"Good money?" asked Doug.

"No. Terrible. It was great though."

"The girls, though. They must have been all over you."

"No. Not really."

"Well, you must be glad to be doing what you're doing now."

Andrew didn't answer. He was staring at the Steinway thinking, "Why did I turn the conversation to those days, sneaking out when dad was passed out in front of the TV, or on the front porch, or in the bathtub with his clothes on."

Those bars. Andrew was a boy in the company of men, hard men, knocked around but still standing, men who were living testimonies to a philosophy of surviving, men who could drink all night without hitting their wife or falling asleep in a bathtub. Why had his father gotten into that bathtub? That never made any sense.

Not just drink for these men either. Heroin in the bathroom; neckties tied around biceps. Cocaine on women's compacts, cut into lines with stray razors. Somehow, these men let Andrew into their lives. Murphy, Legman, Samuel Batiste, Little Man Sullivan, Oglesby. But mostly Murphy.

Andrew stood. "It's late. I need to call my wife."

In his room, Andrew uncapped his Laphroaig to let it breathe and phoned his Sarah. She answered the phone on the third ring.

"Hi baby," said Andrew. "I missed you today."

"Hmmm," said Sarah, doing something in the kitchen that involved the clatter of plates. "I missed you too. How's it going?"

"Same boring conference. Same faces as every other year. One speaker—I must have heard his same speech four-five times."

"Next conference, you tell your boss you can't go. Tell him your wife needs you."

Andrew smiled. "How are the girls?"

"Good. Adrienne told me she was going to recycle her New Year's resolutions from last year because recycling is good."

Andrew smiled again.

"Andrew. Murphy passed."

"What's that?" asked Andrew.

"Your friend Murphy died. It was in the papers today. Angina something something. I clipped it out of the paper for you. The service is Tuesday."

Andrew felt calm, as if he already knew somehow. "I'm surprised you remembered his name. You only met him, what, that one time."

"You loved that old man, though. I was jealous the way you talked about him, when you told some story about those pool halls. Of course, I remember him."

There was a silence. Even the dishes stopped clattering.

"The girls are calling. I gotta go. Goodnight Andrew. I love you. Sorry about Murphy."

"I love you too."

Andrew hung up the phone and sat on the edge of the bed. Somewhere in the night, somewhere in the storm, Murphy swirled like smoke, not gone yet, but going. Andrew was sure he would grieve when Murphy was finally gone. He had haunted Andrew all day. It made perfect sense now. He had followed him in the wisp of Davis' "Valentine" he heard downtown, in the vapors of Dexter Gordon that Andrew had heard in traffic. Murphy had watched from darkened windows and closed elevator doors. He had waited in that corner pocket room of the Trenton hotel with the silent upright Steinway. Murphy had woken memories in Andrew, reminding him all day of how he had escaped his dad and how much he loved music.

It all made sense. Murphy would have haunted him, if it was possible, but only for a day, just to show that he could. Just like everything Murphy did. Music, women, pool, poker, tonk, dominos, his on-again-off-again education of the young Mr. Andrew: Murphy would take a fiery interest for a day or two, then fade back into a corner with his bourbon for days, always fading after a strong showing. Tomorrow, or sometime tonight, Andrew was sure Murphy would drift away into death, his point proved, saying "So there. Don't think I can't come back, either."

Andrew could smell his opened bottle of Laphroaig as it breathed into the room. Every year, as Scotch ages, about 2% evaporates. The brewers call this the angel's dram, or angel's portion. Andrew felt like his life had slowly evaporated away, 2% a year. This research job was supposed to be for one year, then go to school for music. But then a year became two, then three, and then Adrienne came and little Dee and then, all of a sudden, he was sitting in a hotel room listening to Sarah say that Murphy is dead. His life with Murphy had evaporated. Is it called the angel's dram because it is the best portion? Could it be regained, impossibly snatched from the air? Is there time to reclaim the shape of my life by putting the old dents back in?

The room seemed close and stifling. Andrew looked out the window. Somebody Flood was right; there was a bookstore across the street. Andrew had this feeling about bookstores—that they were powder kegs, ready to amplify whatever emotion you have when you enter one. If you were happy, you felt happier. If you felt melancholy, you felt sadder. Andrew didn't want to stay in his room, but in the mood he was in he couldn't cross the street to the bookstore for fear of what would happen. He took his room key and wallet and walked into the hall. He felt Murphy watching him, but it was probably just how the storm slapped at the windows.

Down a flight of stairs and he popped out on a landing overlooking the lobby. Doug Man of Cheviots passed him on his way to his room with a 45-year old researcher whose nametag read "Annie." Doug stared at Andrew without recognition. Was he drunk? Forgetful? It made Andrew feel like he was the ghost today, not Murphy.

Piano music drifted from the room in the corner pocket. The song might have been "The Very Thought of You," but Andrew could only catch a little over the crowd and the storm. It wasn't Murphy playing, of course, but Andrew refused to go and see because, if Murphy wasn't the ghost haunting him, then it was the ghost of his past life, or maybe his possible life, haunting the life he was actually living—a ghost made up not just of ectoplasm and willfulness, but also evaporated Scotch, the insinuation of jazz and the howling of the storm.

Space, or The Last Independent Used Bookstore at the Corner of Warren and Lafayette

Barry Gross

In an aisle that horseshoes the tight space
that can only be occupied one at a time,
among the volume of kindly used books,
I find a floor-to-ceiling column of poetry.

I kneel on the floor,
squint through irregular light,
read faded ink, embossed fabric spines,
thick hardbacks, ragged-edge paper.

From atop footstool,
out-of-reach titles angled and flat,
dust thicker—no recent visitors.
Feels like a perfect moment,
insulated by these words,
keeping traffic, suspicion and the cold at bay.

It's closing time, last call.
The book tender encourages
browsers to purchase.
I'm hoping he overlooks
and locks me in so I can make
a paper blanket of words
to feed this warmth.

The Meaning of the Boy on the Top of the Train

Eric Maywar

I'm going to show you a book and then ask you a question.

The photography book had, on its front cover, a picture of a blur of a boy balancing on top of a speeding train, as if he were surfing; his deep brown eyes staring right at the camera the moment the photograph was shot. In the 80s, poor youth surfed the trains of Brazil.

Not much was inside the book about the boy on the train. There was the name of the photographer (Alex Reyes), the place (Rio de Janeiro), and the date that the photograph was taken.

An old man in Trenton, New Jersey, had purchased this book from that bookstore on Lafayette Street. The picture haunted him. What was the story of this boy? What did the picture mean?

Those of course were two separate questions. Once the photograph was taken, the meaning of the photograph had little to do with the actual story of the boy.

To Alex Reyes of Rio, the photographer, who was able to leverage the picture into some small degree of fame, the picture meant a career as well as a pickup line for impressionable photography majors.

To the bookie Fish Shimmelman of Philadelphia, the picture meant something different. The boy in the photograph lived life on the edge and was a symbol of bravery in the face of a short and uncertain life. He had cut the boy's picture out of a book of photographs and kept it framed on his desk to remind him of the riskiness of the world.

To Nika Hill of London, the boy seemed lonely and haunted. Looking into the boy's piercing eyes fixed in the middle of the blurred photograph, she felt he would have understood why she needed to take her own life.

To Chaneice Clark of Cape Town, the boy was a comfort. To Christine Hayes of Des Moines, he was a figure of desire. To Craig Taylor of Detroit, the boy's irresponsibility filled him with rage. To Raissa Barnes of Seattle, the picture was an example of privileged Americans exploiting the poor by making money from his photograph without paying the boy. To the bookstore owner who sold the book to the old man, the picture (and the book) meant $10.70. To Ed Turner of Anchorage, the boy meant nothing at all.

That was the meaning of the boy, individual meanings to separate people living full and disconnected lives. What was the actual story of the boy? That was a truth that could be known, though truth and meaning were two different things. This is what was happening in the boy's life on the day after that picture was taken.

Julio took a day without surfing. This was the way Julio honored the dead.

Julio had heard about Chavez late last night. He didn't know Chavez well—one of many boys hanging from fences with hands white-knuckled and full of chain-link, waiting for the elevated train to stop. He had seen Chavez, one of many, taking his turn, leap onto the roof of the train with a thump and scramble to the middle, where he would be less likely to fall. Chavez had a lean, hungry face and his eyes had been small and bright.

Walking past the sun-bleached walls of his neighborhood, Julio felt strange. By this time on any other day, he would be surfing the roofs of elevated trains, moving like lightning above and away from Rio: the air punching his body with heavy cloth fists, his hair aching at the roots as it streamed behind his head. The strong winds would force his eyes shut, but he would know that Rio was still there. He could feel the city under him, surrounding him like a dark cloud, kept away only by the winds of the speeding train. Instead, today, in honor of Chavez, Julio walked deep in the heart of Rio where everything was close and slow moving. Having nowhere to go, he walked to his sister's house.

Maria was six months pregnant. When her brother entered the front room, she was eating a raw onion for luck. Tears ran down her face washing all the bad luck from her eyes. When Maria saw her brother, her face darkened as if a cloud had passed between it and the sun. She knew the only thing that would keep Julio from riding the trains was the death of another surfer.

Julio pulled the cross from under his shirt and held its smooth metal in his hand. He avoided Maria's eyes, watching instead a fly as it made its way through the room.

"Another boy has died?" Maria asked. "How many deaths do you need to mourn before you stop? When I mourn for you, it will be longer than one day."

Maria and Julio were having two different conversations and didn't know it. All afternoon, Maria had been thinking about the father of her child, who had disappeared months ago and how she was not free to do the same. She could not disappear from the child growing within her. Men move so easily, she thought. They can escape the past, where women cannot. Women are tied to their past as if with a leash.

It was with these thoughts she had asked, "When will you face life and come down from the tops of trains?"

Julio sat, his fingers twisting the cross' chain in agitation. What was he to do? He wanted his sister to understand what this meant to him. He knew she was afraid he would be the next surfer thrown to the ground by the strong wires that cut through the air, or by an unexpected jump of a speeding train. But he could not stop surfing. The trains were magic, and the winds kept away the blood and dirt of Rio. Only up there was he alive. How could he make her understand that?

"Here on the ground, the air is heavy," he said. "Like a weight. But up there, the air is so good."

Maria turned from Julio. She put a hand on the swelling in her stomach and closed her eyes. She imagined the father of her child thinking the same thing the night he disappeared: that Maria's love was a like a weight and that he needed to find a place where the air was good.

She did not turn to Julio because now she was ashamed of her tears. She did not speak to Julio because Julio was young, and a man, and she would forever be on the margin of his understanding.

If these two people who shared a father and a mother and a home and a childhood could look at one event and see two different meanings, it is no wonder that a thousand people with a thousand contexts read a thousand different meanings into the picture of a boy on the top of a train. Does this infinite fracturing of meaning drive you mad? Does it energize you? Or do you ignore it and go about your life knowing that your interpretation is true?

Biographies

ILENE DUBE covers the arts scene in Mercer and Bucks counties for The Artful Blogger. Her writing has appeared in *Hyperallergic, Sculpture Magazine, Princeton Magazine,* and many others. She lives in Princeton Junction, New Jersey.

JEFF EDELSTEIN is a columnist for *The Trentonian,* an instructor at Rider University, and a radio host on NJ 101.5. He lives in New Jersey.

BARRY GROSS' collections of poetry include *Coiled Logic* and *Angled Portraits.* He lives in Bucks County, Pennsylvania, and frequently travels across the Delaware River to Trenton, to find pre-owned books and poetry readings at Classics Books.

JOHN GUMMERE grew up in Trenton, and graduated from Columbia University and the Pennsylvania Academy of the Fine Arts. He is a graphic designer, illustrator, and painter based in Morrisville, Pennsylvania.

YUSEF KOMUNYAKAA won the 1994 Pulitzer Prize for Poetry. He received his MFA from University of California, Irvine. His collections of poetry include *Copacetic, I Apologize for the Eyes in My Head, Dien Cai Dau, Taboo, Pleasure Dome, Talking Dirty to the Gods, Thieves of Paradise, Neon Vernacular, The Emperor of Water Clocks* and *Magic City.* He teaches poetry at New York University and lives in Trenton, New Jersey.

DOC LONG attended Columbia University and the College of New Jersey. His collections of poetry include *Rules for Cool* and *Timbuktu Blues*. He is retired and lives in Trenton, New Jersey.

ERIC MAYWAR received his MFA from Western Michigan University. He is the author of the novel *Running Flat*. He owns Classics Books (that used bookshop on Lafayette) with his wife Donna Maywar. He lives in Trenton, New Jersey.

LEON RAINBOW is a graffiti artist and curator of Jersey Fresh Jam graffiti arts festival. He lives in Trenton, New Jersey.

JACKIE REINSTEDLER lives in Anchorage, Alaska.

NANCY SCOTT has had more than 400 poems published in over 100 journals and anthologies and is the author of *Down to the Quick, One Stands Guard, One Sleeps, The Owl Prince* and *Ah, Men*. She is the managing editor of *U.S. 1 Worksheets* and lives in Lawrenceville, New Jersey.

TOM WEBSTER received his MFA from Western Michigan University. He has been published in *Amaranthus* and *The Kalamazoo Reader*. He lives in Kalamazoo, Michigan.

DAVID LEE WHITE received his MFA from University of Pittsburgh. His plays include *Fixed, Blood: A Comedy, Panther Hollow, Trenton Lights, The Festival Quartet* and *Rocket Sex Magic*. He was Associate Artistic Director of Passage Theatre for 14 years, teaches theater at Rider University and Drexel University and currently resides in New Jersey.

CPSIA information can be obtained
at www.ICGtesting.com
Printed in the USA
FSHW021828140619

9 781933 974323